Living in the 1940s

Rosemary Rees & Judith Maguire

Heinemann

Heinemann Library,
an imprint of Heinemann Publishers (Oxford) Ltd,
Halley Court, Jordan Hill, Oxford, OX2 8EJ

OXFORD LONDON EDINBURGH
MADRID PARIS ATHENS BOLOGNA
MELBOURNE SYDNEY AUCKLAND
SINGAPORE TOKYO IBADAN
NAIROBI GABORONE HARARE
PORTSMOUTH NH (USA)

First published 1993
93 94 95 96 10 9 8 7 6 5 4 3 2 1

British Library Cataloguing in Publication Data
is available on request from the British Library.

ISBN 0 431 07217 5

Designed by Philip Parkhouse
Printed and bound in China

Acknowledgements
The authors and publisher would like to thank the following
for permission to reproduce photographs:
Hulton Picture Company: pp. 5, 6, 7, 8, 9, 10, 11, 13, 15,
16, 17, 19, 20, 21, 23, 25, 28, 30,
Imperial War Museum: p. 26
Magnum Photos/George Rodger: pp. 4, 14, 22
Popperfoto: p. 24; Topham: pp. 12, 18, 27

Cover photograph: Hulton Picture Company

Contents

Home 1

Britain was at war with Germany for nearly six years.
Many homes were bombed during the war.
This man tried to save some of the furniture from his house.
Life was very different during the war.

Many towns were bombed during the war.
Children were sent to live in the country, to keep them safe.
Moving children was called evacuating them.
The children did not know who they would live with.

Home 2

Many people had air-raid shelters in their gardens.
A siren sounded to tell them the bombs were going to drop. When they heard the siren, everyone went to the nearest air-raid shelter.
Sometimes people had to spend all night in the shelter.

During the war, some food was very difficult to get.
This family grew their own fruit and vegetables.
People worked hard to grow food for themselves and for the soldiers who were away fighting.

Home 3

Some foods were difficult to get, so they were rationed.
Everyone had a ration book, which told you how much food you could have for a week.
Foods like cheese, eggs and milk were rationed, and so were soap and sweets.

Sometimes, women had to stand in line for hours to get food for their families. Even though food was rationed, it sometimes ran out.

Some food, like bananas and tinned fish, were hardly ever in the shops.

School 1

When the bombs dropped, children had lessons in the air-raid shelter.
The air-raid shelter had no windows. There was no broken glass in the shelter if a bomb went off.
Children were safe in the shelters.
In school children practised air-raid drill as well as fire drill.

Everyone had to carry a gas mask during the war. A gas mask helped you breathe if gas bombs were dropped.

Children carried them over their shoulders in a box.

Babies were too small to wear gas masks. They had special carrycots.

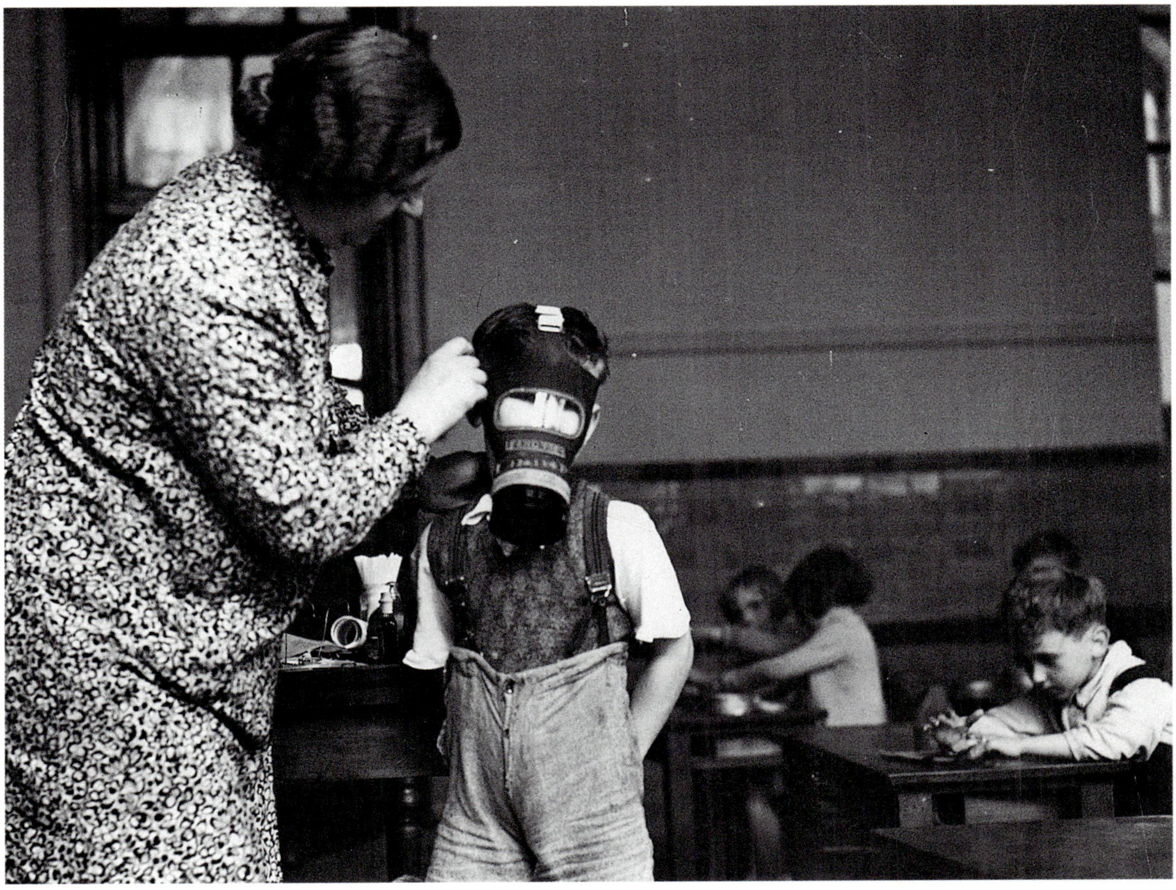

School 2

These children were waiting to get on a train.
They were going to stay in the countryside.
It was safer there.
They went back home when the war was over.

At school these boys learnt to knit and to read and write.
They knitted scarves for the soldiers who were fighting in the war.
Lots of children went to all-girl or all-boy schools.
Children had to go to school until they were 15.

Work 1

These men were air-raid wardens.
They helped at houses that were bombed.
They looked for people who were hurt in the rubble.
Sometimes the buildings were on fire.
Air-raid wardens tried to make the buildings safe.

These women worked in an office.
It was bombed three times.
The building was not safe, so they had to work outside on the grass.
They did not use computers.
They used typewriters.
Typewriters did not use electricity.

Work 2

This woman worked in a factory making guns.
Before the war, most women looked after their children at home.
During the war, a lot of the men went away to fight.
The women went to the factories to do the jobs the men had left.

Women were also needed to work on the land.
They were called the Women's Land Army.
Women learnt to do lots of things they could not do before the war.
These women learnt to drive a tractor.

Spare Time 1

These boys played at being soldiers.
They had wooden guns, but carried real gas masks.
A lot of toys were hand-made during the war. Factories were busy making guns, bullets and tanks.
Many toys were handed down to younger brothers or sisters.

These children were evacuated to the country from the city.
They played in the fields and picked blackberries.
They were not afraid of the bombs.
Many children had lots of fun living in the country.

Spare time 2

Children did lots of things we do now, like drawing.
They played games like chess and ludo. They did not have computer games.
This little girl had rags in her hair to make it curly. What would you use to make your hair curly?

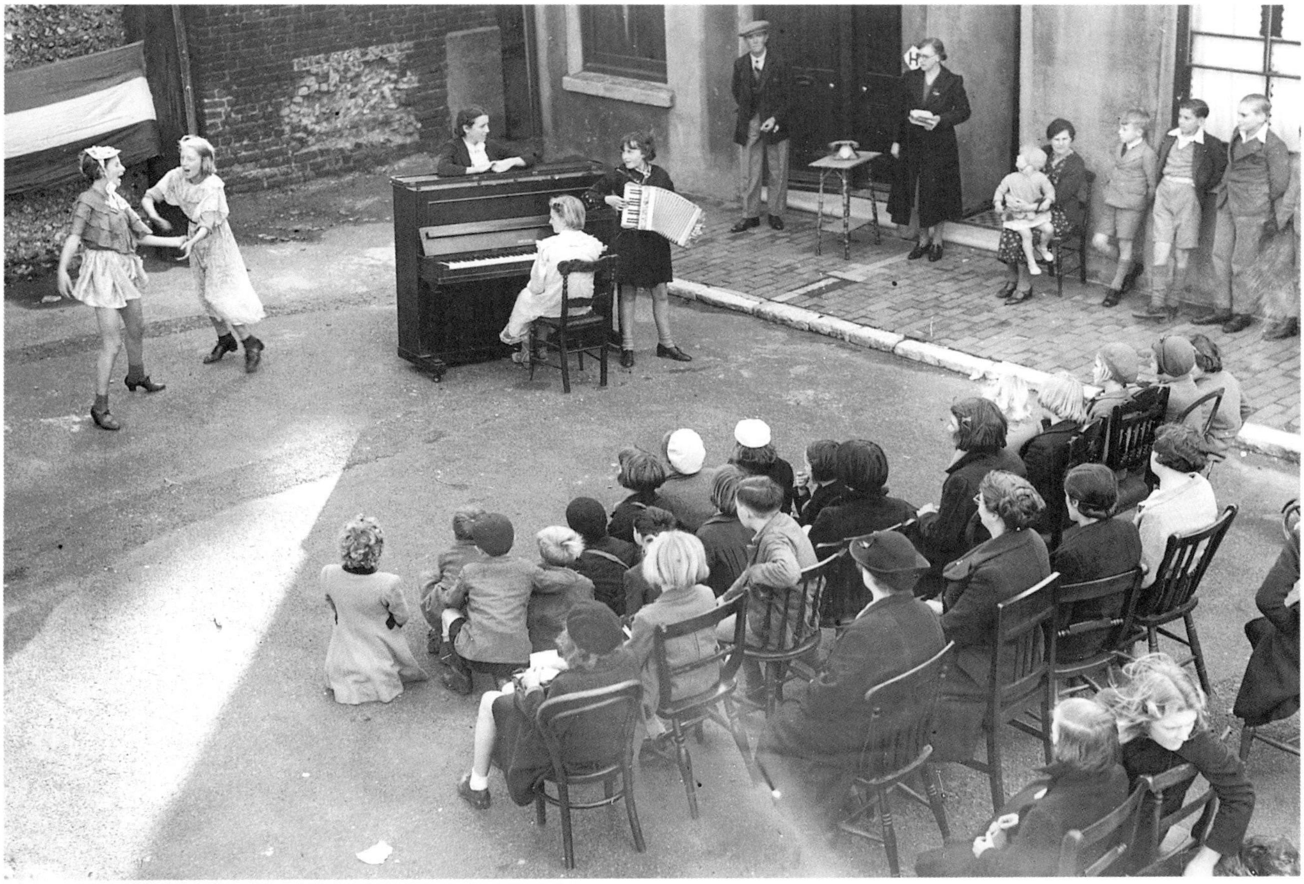

Many cinemas and theatres had been bombed.
These girls gave concerts in the street.
The girls raised money to help pay for new aeroplanes for the soldiers.
They raised a lot of money.

Spare time 3

People in the cities spent a lot of time in the air-raid shelters.
They took things with them to do, so that they did not get bored.
Some people did their knitting.
Children played with toys.

People still tried to have fun, even if there was a war.
They really enjoyed themselves when the soldiers and sailors came home on leave.
Everyone knew the men had to go back to the fighting.
They wanted to enjoy themselves when they could.

Holidays 1

Christmas was a very special time.
Everyone hoped the war would be over by Christmas.
Many children did not see their parents at Christmas, because they had been sent to live in the country.
People saved their ration books to have a lot of food on Christmas day.

These girls could not play on the beach.
The barbed wire stopped them.
Many beaches had bombs hidden on them, to stop the Germans landing.
If you went to a safe beach, it was very crowded.

Holidays 2

This poster tried to get people to have their holidays on a farm.
It was fun to stay on a farm, but it was hard work.
There were many jobs to do.
The cows had to be milked, corn had to be cut and the chickens had to be fed.

Lots of older children went to work on farms in the school holidays.
The food they grew was used to feed people who were in hospital.
Some people in hospital had been hurt by bombs.
Soldiers hurt in the war were also looked after in hospital.

Special Days 1

These people got married during the war. Sometimes people got married quickly, because they had to go back to the fighting.

Material for wedding dresses was hard to buy.

Sometimes women made their dresses from parachute silk.

This baby was christened in
the 1940s.
All of the family wanted to be there.
Some of the men were not there.
They were fighting in the war.
It was a very special time when a
new baby arrived.

Special Days 2

This street party was held to celebrate the end of the war.
They did not have special food, because food was still rationed
People were very happy that the war was over.
They wanted to share this special time with all their friends.

Time Line

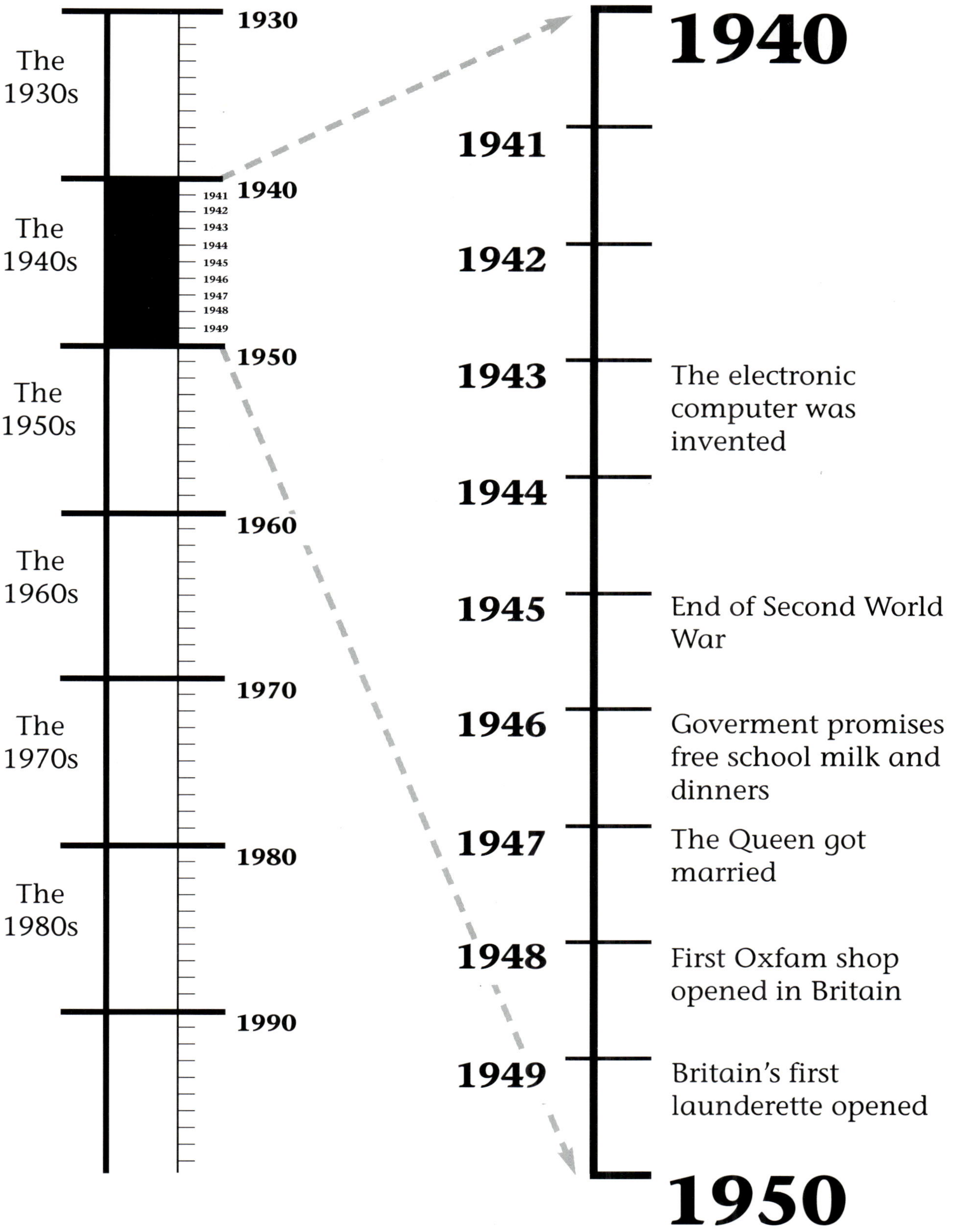
1930
The 1930s
1940
The 1940s
1941
1942
1943
1944
1945
1946
1947
1948
1949
1950
The 1950s
1960
The 1960s
1970
The 1970s
1980
The 1980s
1990
1940
1941
1942
1943
The electronic computer was invented
1944
1945
End of Second World War
1946
Goverment promises free school milk and dinners
1947
The Queen got married
1948
First Oxfam shop opened in Britain
1949
Britain's first launderette opened
1950

Index